The Library of Author Biographies™

Scott O'Dell

The Library of Author Biographies™

Scott O'Dell

Simone Payment

The Rosen Publishing Group, Inc., New York

The author would like to thank Marina Lang for her suggestions on the manuscript. She would also like to thank the reference librarians of Wakefield (Massachusetts) Public Library for their assistance.

Published in 2006 by The Rosen Publishing Group, Inc.
29 East 21st Street, New York, NY 10010

Library of Congress Cataloging-in-Publication Data

Payment, Simone.
Scott O'Dell / by Simone Payment.
    p. cm.—(The library of author biographies)
Includes bibliographical references and index.
ISBN 1-4042-0467-9 (lib. bdg.)
ISBN 1-4042-0651-5 (pbk. bdg.)
1. O'Dell, Scott, 1898–1989. 2. Authors, American—20th century—Biography. 3. Young adult fiction—Authorship. 4. Historical fiction—Authorship. 5. Children's stories—Authorship.
I. Title. II. Series.
PS3529.D434Z85 2005
813'.54—dc22

                                                                   2004023240

Manufactured in the United States of America

Table of Contents

Introduction:
A Writer with
a Message

"Always, I knew I would be a writer,"[1] Scott O'Dell said once. A lover of books from the time he was a very young child, O'Dell would eventually become "probably the foremost American writer of children's historical fiction of the latter half of the twentieth century,"[2] according to his biographer David Russell.

O'Dell wrote books and newspaper articles all of his life, but it wasn't until he published his first book for children in 1960—when he was sixty-two years old—that his writing career truly began. *Island of the Blue Dolphins*, about a young woman stranded alone on an island for eighteen years, was an enormous success. It won several literary awards, including the Newbery Medal, the top American award given to a children's book. Although the book was published more than forty years ago, *Island of the Blue Dolphins* is still one of the ten top-selling books for children and continues to sell more than 100,000 copies per year. Most critics agree that it is O'Dell's best book, and John Rowe Townsend, a children's author himself, said, "Among all the Newbery Medal winners there are few better books."[3]

Named Odell Gabriel Scott when he was born in Los Angeles, California, in 1898, he changed his name in the 1920s after a newspaper mistakenly printed his name as "Scott O'Dell." He grew up in small towns in and around Los Angeles, learning to love the ocean, the mountains, and the landscape of what was then a frontier town. He was an avid reader and an excellent student. After high school, O'Dell went to three colleges in the United States and one in Italy, although he never graduated from any of them. He didn't think his college courses would help his writing career.

In his early career, O'Dell wrote stories for newspapers, worked in the movie business as a cameraman and a script reviewer, and was even a citrus farmer. All along, though, he knew he wanted to be a writer. His first book, which was about analyzing screenplays (or photoplays, as they were called at the time), was published in 1924. He went on to write several novels for adults, but it wasn't until *Island of the Blue Dolphins* was published that he discovered his true calling—writing children's books.

After 1960, with the success of *Island of the Blue Dolphins*, O'Dell no longer wrote books for adults. Instead, he wrote twenty-five more books for children and young adults, beginning with *The King's Fifth*, his second young adult novel. Published in 1966, it earned a Newbery Honor, as well as several other awards and praise from critics and readers. *The Black Pearl*, published a year later, also won a Newbery Honor.

These first three young adult books by O'Dell were written about historical topics, and they "established O'Dell's reputation as a writer of first-rate historical fiction,"[4] wrote David Russell. They also helped make historical fiction popular again. After World War II (1939–1945), not many novels for children had focused on history, but after O'Dell's three successful historical novels, many authors began focusing on this genre.

Later in his career, O'Dell encouraged other authors to write about history for young adults by establishing the Scott O'Dell Award for Historical Fiction in 1982. Each year, a $5,000 prize is awarded to an American author who has written a book of historical fiction set in North or South America.

Before O'Dell began writing for children in 1960, few books for young adults had featured female characters, but O'Dell changed that model with his portrayal of Karana, the heroine in *Island of the Blue Dolphins*. Karana is a strong, resourceful girl who not only learns to survive on her own, but overcomes her loneliness and goes on to live a happy life with only the island animals and sea creatures to keep her company. Many of O'Dell's other books feature strong young women, such as *Sing Down the Moon*; *Sarah Bishop*; and *Streams to the River, River to the Sea: A Novel of Sacagawea*.

O'Dell once said, "I have only done things that I've been really enthusiastic about, stories that have stirred me."[5] He was an excellent storyteller, and most of his novels are interesting and fast-paced. However, O'Dell also used his novels to send messages that were important to him. One of the lessons he hoped readers would learn from his books was the importance of preserving the environment and nature. Many of his novels speak out about the mistreatment of animals, and he hoped that his books would teach people to have respect for the natural world. O'Dell strongly believed that humans are not superior to animals, and he makes this point especially strongly in *Island of the Blue Dolphins*.

Another message O'Dell hoped to send with his novels was that although people may be very different on the outside, we are very much alike on the inside. O'Dell's main characters are of many different races and backgrounds, and he hoped to show that we should respect each other and be sensitive to our differences.

O'Dell was particularly unhappy about the way Native Americans had been treated by the Europeans when the Europeans first came to America. He used several of his novels, including *Sing Down the Moon*, which won a 1971 Newbery Honor, to speak out against the mistreatment of Native Americans.

O'Dell felt that much of this mistreatment came as the result of greed for money and power. This message is especially powerful in *The King's Fifth*. *The Black Pearl* and *The Treasure of Topo-el-Bampo* are just two of O'Dell's other books that speak out against the destructiveness of greed.

In the late 1960s, after writing his string of three prize-winning historical novels, O'Dell began to branch out and focus on different topics and settings. He wrote two books for elementary-school children, a book detailing his trip up the California coast on a fifty-foot (fifteen-meter) sailboat, and several novels set in the present day.

Throughout the 1970s and 1980s, O'Dell wrote about one book a year. Although none was as successful as his earliest works for children, David Russell said, "We can justly admire a writer who refuses to stagnate and sink into complacency, but who approaches each new project with daring and a sense of adventure. It was a spirit that kept Scott O'Dell vibrant for over 90 years."[6]

In addition to his Newbery Medal and three Newbery Honors, O'Dell won numerous other awards. In 1972, O'Dell received the Hans Christian Andersen Award in honor of his career to that point. At the time, he was only the second American writer to receive this major international award. O'Dell received several other lifetime achievement awards and continued to write books until his death in 1989. His last book, *My Name Is Not Angelica*, was published the year O'Dell died, when he was ninety-one years old.

Scott O'Dell was honored to have spent the second half of his life writing for young adults.

He said that they want "to know what it is to be good and truthful and fair, kind and courageous."[7] He respected his readers and the characters in his novels. Scott O'Dell's stories have much to teach us.

1 Early Years in a Frontier Town

L ong before Los Angeles, California, became the movie capital in the world, it was a quiet frontier town of the western United States. Scott O'Dell said in an autobiographical sketch that there were "more horses than automobiles and more jackrabbits than people"[1] when he was born there on May 23, 1898, as Odell Gabriel Scott.

O'Dell's father, Bennett Mason Scott, and his mother, Mary Elizabeth Scott (née Gabriel), moved to Los Angeles before O'Dell was born. His father worked for the Union Pacific Railroad, and his job kept the family moving often, although never far from Los Angeles. The rugged towns in and around Los Angeles and the nearby Pacific Ocean would later become settings for many of O'Dell's stories.

A Young Adventurer

The family, including O'Dell's younger sister, Lucile, moved to San Pedro when O'Dell was eight. San Pedro, which was part of the city of Los Angeles, was on the Pacific Ocean, and one of O'Dell's homes there was built on stilts at the edge of the water. On O'Dell's first day in San Pedro, he went to the harbor with other boys from his street. In his book *Cruise of the Arctic Star*, O'Dell describes how he stood on the pier while the other boys prepared to swim:

> I had never been in water more than waist-deep before and I had never swum, unless flailing your arms while crouching with one foot firmly on the bottom can be called swimming. But how could I confess this to the boys who lived on Elm Street, the street I had just moved into, who I hoped would be my friends someday?[2]

O'Dell considered telling the other boys that he had a stomachache or that he couldn't swim, but he decided that he'd rather keep his dignity and drown than take either of those options. So he "jumped and fell through the air holding [his] breath, [his] eyes closed, too scared to pray. It was not a dive of any sort, nor was it graceful."[3]

He quickly made his way to the ladder and scrambled up to the pier. No one gave him good marks for his leap off the pier, but he guessed "everyone was just happy that the new boy . . . had not drowned."[4]

O'Dell's adventures with his new friends in San Pedro continued over the next few years. Each Saturday morning, they explored the hills above San Pedro, learning about the wildlife there. They caught, skinned, roasted, and then ate squirrels, a meal for which O'Dell never developed a taste. They captured lizards and snakes and sometimes would find owls hiding from the sun in small holes. They would pull the startled owls out of the holes and wring their necks, just because they could. O'Dell always remembered this senseless cruelty, and it was part of what led him to write *Island of the Blue Dolphins* many years later.

O'Dell and his friends also went on adventures in the ocean.

> Each of us chose a log from a great raft of logs that were towed into the harbor from the pine forests of Oregon. The logs were twenty feet long or longer, rough with splinters and streaked

with tar. But to us young Magellans they were proud canoes, fashioned by ax and fire, graceful and fierce-prowed, the equals of any storm.

Each of us straddled a log and in single file, using our hands, we paddled to the breakwater and sometimes beyond. Hours later, we returned to the harbor and our waiting mothers.[5]

Out in the harbor, they watched the three-masted ships sail by. They also explored local islands like Dead Man's Island, where they once discovered a skeleton in a cave.

A Life in Books

As a young child, O'Dell loved to be read to. His mother read to him often, and he remembered hounding her to read *Jack and the Beanstalk* over and over again.

My mother must have read it a hundred times. I remember that she would expostulate, "You heard it last night," she'd say, "And the night before and the night before that. I'd think you would get tired of listening." Not me. I sat stolid and silent, certain that she would relent.

And she did. But she began to change events a little to save her sanity, I presume. Jack would sell a pig instead of a cow, plant morning-glory seeds instead of beans, the castle in the sky might have ten turrets instead of two. But one thing she never dared to change was the verse:

Fee, fie, fo, fum!
I smell the blood of an Englishman.
Be he live or be he dead,
I'll grind his bones to make my bread.

That was the one that gave me the shivers. To be honest, it still does.[6]

His mother also read him the fairy tales of Hans Christian Andersen and the Grimm brothers. He recalled, "I heard them at dusk, which is the proper time of day to hear fairy tales. I heard them sitting at my mother's knee, which is the best place, the only place to sit when you leave the safe world you know for the unfamiliar and perilous world you don't know."[7]

As O'Dell grew older, he read classic adventure stories such as *Treasure Island, Robinson Crusoe,* and *Swiss Family Robinson.* He loved these stories so much that he read them many times. Years later, when he began writing *Island of the Blue Dolphins,* he read *Robinson Crusoe* again. "[I wanted] to make certain that what I was writing came from my own research and imagination." O'Dell continued:

[It was a] good idea as it turned out. For one of the dramatic moments in [the] story occurs when Robinson Crusoe discovers Friday's footsteps in the sand. One of the dramatic moments in the story of the Indian girl's eighteen years on the island occurred when the man who rescued her, Captain Nidever, found her footsteps on the beach at Coral Cove. I would have been justified by the facts if I had used this incident. And I debated doing so, but in the end I discarded the idea, for fear of being accused of borrowing.[8]

O'Dell also loved the novels of Sir Walter Scott, the great Scottish writer who happened to be his great-grandmother's cousin. O'Dell's parents gave him a collection of Scott's novels when O'Dell was about ten years old, and he loved it. Scott's historical novels would be a big influence on O'Dell's later writing.

2 A Writer Grows Up

School came very easily to O'Dell and he did well. In fact, at Polytechnic High School in Long Beach, California, O'Dell said he was "the brightest boy—[his] teachers said—they'd ever had or hoped to have."[1]

While O'Dell was in high school, World War I (1914–1918) was raging in Europe, so after he graduated, he joined the army. In the fall of 1918, O'Dell went to Occidental College in Los Angeles for army training. However, World War I ended a few months later, on December 11, so O'Dell was released from the army on December 17, 1918. He decided to stay at Occidental College though for the spring of 1919.

The following year, O'Dell went to the University of Wisconsin and later spent a year at Stanford University back in California. He did not do as well in college as he did in high school. When he went to college, O'Dell said, "I found to my great surprise that I was not the brightest young man in the world. Indeed, I found that most of my classmates were brighter than I was."[2] He went on to explain, "Things had been so easy in elementary school and high school, I hadn't needed to study. What's more, I didn't know how. That's why I wandered around from school to school."[3]

First Publications

Although O'Dell did enjoy his college classes in history and English, he didn't think any of them were helping him in his goal to become a writer. So he decided to quit college and start writing.

Some of O'Dell's early writing was published in local newspapers. When one of his stories was being typeset for the newspaper, the typesetter reversed O'Dell's given name, Odell Scott, and so it appeared as Scott O'Dell. O'Dell liked the new name so much he decided to keep it and changed his name officially.

In the early 1920s, O'Dell went to work for the Palmer Photoplay Company. His job was to evaluate photoplays (now known as screenplays) for silent movies. O'Dell also began teaching photoplay writing through a mail-order course. His experience teaching this course led to his first book, called *Representative Photoplays Analyzed*, which was published in 1924. He wrote it while working for the Paramount Motion Picture Studio as a technical director.

O'Dell continued to work for movie companies in Los Angeles. He also worked in Rome, Italy, as a cameraman filming the original, silent version of the movie *Ben Hur*. "We shot thousands of feet of film in Rome," said O'Dell. "But none of it was ever used. After months of hard work, surprises, and disasters, [the crew] went back to the United States, and the film was shot on the back lots of Hollywood."[4]

O'Dell, however, decided to stay in Italy, where he took classes at the University of Rome. He also lived in Florence, Italy, for a while. It was there that he wrote his first novel, called *Pinfeathers*. O'Dell later said that it was appropriate that it was called *Pinfeathers* "because [the writing style] was very young and fuzzy."[5] He took his novel back to California with him when he returned in 1927 and rewrote the whole thing, but he wasn't happy with it and burned it.

With his writing career temporarily on the back burner, O'Dell held many different jobs back in California. He did more work in the movie business, worked at a stockbroker's office, and even became a citrus farmer for a time.

First Novels

O'Dell also continued to write in his spare time, and in 1934, his first novel was published. Called *Woman of Spain: A Story of Old California*, it tells the story of the daughter of Spanish immigrants living in northern California. Parts of the book are based on stories he heard while working in the orange groves in Pomona Valley, California.

The protagonist is a strong young woman who would serve as a model for later female characters in O'Dell novels, including Karana in *Island of the Blue Dolphins*, and the main characters in *Alexandra* and *Sarah Bishop*. According to David Russell, these women "must fight their own battles with little help from anyone . . . and are fearless, both physically and emotionally strong, independent, and determined."[6]

The Metro-Goldwyn-Mayer company (MGM) paid O'Dell $24,000 for the rights to make *Woman of Spain* into a movie. This was a lot of money at the time, and it helped O'Dell get through several years when much of the rest of the United States was struggling financially from the Great Depression.

O'Dell did not sell too many copies of his first novel. When *Woman of Spain* was published, a bookstore in San Francisco invited him to speak and do a book signing. He arrived to find that only thirty-two people had come to the event. He began his talk but later admitted, "There is nothing worse than an author's speech, especially the author of a first book."[7]

After his speech, fifteen people bought copies of the book, and O'Dell was left looking at the other eighty-five copies sitting on the table. Luckily, a man stepped up and asked O'Dell to autograph the remaining eighty-five copies. This generous man later gave the books to schools, prisons, hospitals, and retirement homes in San Francisco.

O'Dell's next novel wasn't published until 1947. *Hill of the Hawk* takes place in California during the Mexican-American War (1846–1848). Some of the characters and situations in this novel would later appear in *Carlota*, one of his children's novels, which was published in 1977.

Also in 1947, O'Dell got a job reviewing books for the *Los Angeles Daily News*. He published stories in other newspapers as well, and he continued to write in his spare time. O'Dell's book *Country of the Sun, Southern California: An Informal History and Guide* was published in 1957. The book was a guide to the places O'Dell had lived throughout most of his life and was filled with stories of the history of Southern California.

O'Dell's last novel for adults, *The Sea Is Red*, was published in 1958. This book tells the story of the Confederate ship the *Alabama*, which would later be the subject of O'Dell's children's novel called *The 290*, which was published in 1976. *The Sea Is Red*, just like the rest of O'Dell's books for adults, was not very successful. At the time that *The Sea Is Red* was published, O'Dell was already sixty years old. He might have decided to retire or to try something new, but he didn't. Just a few years later, his writing career took an unexpected and rewarding turn.

3 Success: *Island of the Blue Dolphins*

One of Scott O'Dell's biographers, Malcolm Usrey, described *Island of the Blue Dolphins* as "O'Dell's masterpiece and one of a half dozen or so great historical novels for children by an American writer in the past two or three decades."[1] O'Dell had been a writer for almost forty years when he began *Island of the Blue Dolphins*. Although he didn't plan for it to be a children's book, *Island of the Blue Dolphins* is still recognized today as one of the best historical novels for young adults. The book brought together many of O'Dell's interests—history, the environment, adventure, and survival. It also featured a strong young woman as the protagonist, which was unusual at a time when most books were written about or for boys.

A Legend Sparks O'Dell's Imagination

O'Dell began writing *Island of the Blue Dolphins* in the late 1950s, while he was still working for the *Los Angeles Daily News*. He came across the subject for the book years before. While doing research for his book about the history of Southern California, he learned the story of the Lost Woman of San Nicolas.

The woman was part of a small tribe of Native Americans living on the island of San Nicolas, about 75 miles (121 kilometers) southwest of Los Angeles. When the tribe was being taken to the California mainland on a ship, the young woman jumped overboard to return to her baby, who had been left behind. (However, in O'Dell's book, the main character jumped overboard to return for her brother, not her baby.)

Left alone on the island from 1835 to 1853, the young woman had to fend for herself. Found after eighteen years, the young woman was unable to communicate with her rescuers or others at the mission she was taken to because no one spoke her language. She died a few years later and was buried at the Santa Barbara Mission in California.

O'Dell had always been intrigued with this legend and decided to write his version of the young woman's story. From the barest details, according to David Russell, he "constructed [a] story of courage, loneliness, and the need for love and understanding in the world."[2] Since O'Dell did not set out to write this book for children, he said that he "didn't know what young people were reading and . . . didn't consider [*Island of the Blue Dolphins*] a children's book, necessarily."[3]

When O'Dell finished writing the book, he sent it to his literary agents. They suggested that he change the heroine—Karana—to a boy "because girls were only interested in romance and such." O'Dell continued, "This seemed silly to me. So I picked up the story, went to New York City, and gave it to my editor, who accepted it the next day."[4]

Karana's Story

In O'Dell's version of the legend of the Lost Woman of San Nicolas, the story is told through the eyes of Karana, a member of the small tribe of Native Americans who were the only inhabitants of the island. When Aleuts arrive on the island to hunt for sea otters, Karana's father, the chief of the tribe, welcomes the visitors. He makes a deal with them that allows them to hunt the sea otters living in the waters surrounding the island in exchange for beads and other trinkets. Karana grows worried, fearing that the Aleuts will kill all the sea otters, whom she considers her friends. Karana's fears are realized. Not only do the Aleuts kill most of the sea otters, they also kill Karana's father and many other men of the island.

With much of the tribe now dead, the remaining inhabitants are worried about surviving on the island. The new chief of the tribe sails to the mainland in a canoe and returns with a large ship to take all of Karana's people to the mainland.

As the tribe is boarding the ship, Karana realizes that her brother has gone back for his spear. Not wanting to leave him behind, she jumps overboard and swims to shore. However, the ship leaves without them, and Karana and her brother, Ramo, are abandoned on the island.

Soon after, wild dogs kill Ramo, so Karana must now survive on her own. She learns to make weapons for hunting and protection, something women of her tribe were not taught to do. She gathers food and stores it for the upcoming winter. After she decides that living in her old village makes her feel too lonely, she builds herself a new shelter.

In her first few months alone on the island, Karana believes a ship will return for her. However, no ship arrives.

> The thought of being alone on the island while so many suns rose from the sea and went slowly back down filled my heart with loneliness. I had not felt so lonely before because I was sure the ship would return . . . Now my hopes were dead. Now I was really alone. I could not eat much, nor could I sleep without dreaming terrible dreams.[5]

Karana decides to try to leave the island. She repairs one of the tribe's old canoes, loads it with food, and begins paddling east.

> . . . a swarm of dolphins appeared. They came swimming out of the west, but as they saw the canoe they turned around in a great circle and began to follow me. They swam up slowly and so close that I could see their eyes, which are large and the color of the ocean. Then they swam on ahead of the canoe, crossing back and forth in front of it, diving in and out, as if they were weaving a piece of cloth with their broad snouts.

> Dolphins are animals of good omen. It made me happy to have them swimming around the canoe, and though my hands had begun to bleed from the chafing of the paddle, just watching them made me forget the pain. I was

very lonely before they appeared, but now I felt that I had friends with me and did not feel the same.[6]

Karana's attempt to leave the island is not successful. Her canoe begins to leak, and after a dark night at sea, she turns around and heads back to the island. On her way back, she plans how she will repair the canoe and try again. However, when she reaches the island, Karana realizes she has learned something.

> I was happy to be home. Everything that I saw—the otter playing in the kelp, the rings of foam around the rocks that guarded the harbor, the gulls flying, the tides moving past the sandspit—filled me with happiness.
>
> I was surprised that I felt this way, for it was only a short time ago that I had stood on this same rock and felt that I could not bear to live here another day . . . Now I knew that I would never go again.
>
> The Island of the Blue Dolphins was my home; I had no other.[7]

Karana makes peace with the fact that she is alone on the island, but soon she befriends one of the wild dogs there. She names him Rontu, and he becomes her friend and companion. She talks to him all day long and he looks at her, cocking his head to one side and then another, as if he understands her words. "Because of this I was not lonely,"[8] she says.

Karana befriends other island creatures as well and begins to respect nature. She comes to believe that "animals and birds are like people, too, though they do not talk the same or do the same things. Without them the earth would be an unhappy place."[9]

Life on the island continues for Karana and Rontu. Some days are filled with danger and excitement, such as the day Karana tries to spear an enormous devilfish, or giant manta ray. Other days, Karana and Rontu wander peacefully around the island, enjoying the summer sun or searching for food.

Many years pass in this way, until Rontu dies. His death seems like another cruel blow for Karana, but somehow, as the writer Carolyn T. Kingston put it, Karana "goes on, milking from her harsh environment what companionship and beauty it offers. She makes of her island something more than a prison and has moments of joy."[10]

Eighteen years after Karana is abandoned, a ship comes to the island and she is rescued. The book ends as Karana sails away from the island with dolphins leaping in front of the boat.

A Unique Book

Island of the Blue Dolphins is much more than a survival story. According to critic John Rowe Townsend, it is the story of a "strong, sensible, intelligent, resourceful"[11] young woman who learns important life lessons. Karana faces a very harsh environment and must face it alone. She makes the best of her circumstances, though, and comes to lead a happy life.

In the years before the women's equality movement of the early 1970s, a strong female heroine in a children's novel was unusual. The fact that the main character in *Island of the Blue Dolphins* is a woman was an important part of the story to O'Dell. In this book, and in many of his later novels, he made a conscious effort to portray women as strong. He said, "I am trying to show that women and men do have the same potential."[12]

Island of the Blue Dolphins was also ahead of its time in that it sent a strong environmentalist message. According to David Russell, it was the first "major children's story [to show] the environmentalist's credo—that all life is sacred, that we share this earth together with all living things, and that we have an obligation to preserve the earth intact for succeeding generations."[13] O'Dell said that he "wished to say to the young and to all who wish to listen that we have a chance to come into a new relationship to the things around us."[14] In *Island of the Blue Dolphins*, Karana learns to share her life with the wildlife on the island.

Through *Island of the Blue Dolphins*, O'Dell wanted to teach people to have respect for all forms of life. He had learned much from his early days when he and his friends had hunted—and sometimes killed—wildlife. O'Dell had come to believe that all killing is wrong, and he had developed a great hatred of hunters. In his book *Cruise of the Arctic Star*, he talks about the dwindling number of sea otters due to the actions of humans.

> Otter are gentle creatures, gentle with one another, and great lovers of fun. Along with the dolphin they are the most joyous of all the animals in the sea. It is sad that out of the hundreds of thousands that once inhabited our coast from Alaska to San Nicolas . . . the hunters have left us only a handful.

> And the hunters will leave us fewer of everything, if only they have their way. For all wild things—everything that creeps or walks or flies, whether clothed in fur or feathers—are their target. All the defenseless creatures . . . are at the mercy of this backward group that equates slaughter with manhood.[15]

Rewarded with Awards

Island of the Blue Dolphins was a great success with book critics and with readers. It received the Newbery Medal in 1961. This was a great accomplishment, especially for a book written by an author who had never written a book for children. The book went on to win more than ten other awards in the United States and other countries around the world.

Island of the Blue Dolphins was also made into a movie in 1964. O'Dell was not completely satisfied with the movie because in it, Karana spends only four years on the island. He felt that was not enough time for her character to develop. Nevertheless, the movie was a complement to the success of the book.

O'Dell would never go back to writing for adults and would soon write more award-winning books. *Island of the Blue Dolphins* was just the beginning of a new chapter for O'Dell.

4 Two More Award Winners

With the success of his first book for young adults, Scott O'Dell set out to write more historical novels for young adults. His success continued. O'Dell's next two books—*The King's Fifth* and *The Black Pearl*—won Newbery Honors.

The King's Fifth

The King's Fifth, published in 1966, is considered by some critics to be O'Dell's best book. Set in the early 1500s, it is about the search for gold and the harms that can come from greed.

The story is told from the point of view of Estéban de Sandoval, a young Spanish mapmaker who has taken part in a Spanish expedition to find gold in what is now the American Southwest. When the book begins, Estéban is in prison. Awaiting trial for not handing over one-fifth of the gold found on the expedition to the king of Spain, he tells the story of the trip and how he came to be in prison. The story moves back and forth in time between Estéban's trial and his adventures during the hunt for gold.

When the expedition begins, Estéban's main concern is mapping unknown lands. He is not interested in the prospect of finding gold. Father Francisco, another member of the group, is a Spanish priest who wants to convert the Native Americans there to his religion. Others, including the leader Captain Mendoza, are driven by their hunger for gold and power. Zia, a young Native American girl who serves as their guide and befriends Estéban, is the opposite of Mendoza. She suspects from the start that greed will be their downfall.

It turns out that Zia is right. After the expedition discovers gold, the desire to become rich begins to affect even Estéban. Bad things begin to happen to members of the group. One by one, everyone in the party either leaves or is killed. Estéban does not realize, until it is almost too late, what an effect the gold has had on him. In his book *Twentieth-Century Children's Writers*, D. L. Kirkpatrick describes the end of the expedition:

> . . . Estéban finishes in the Inferno, a hot white sandy basin where his last companion, Father Francisco, dies. And only now does he grasp the enormity of the evil burden and tip the gold, enough to make men rich, into a deep bubbling crater of foul yellow water where it will be lost forever.[1]

Estéban is thrown in prison for not giving the gold to the king of Spain. And at the conclusion of his trial, he is sentenced to three years in jail for his crime. Estéban accepts his sentence because he knows that he has to pay for his greed. Only that will allow him to eventually be free. When his jailer offers him the chance to escape from prison in return for his help in retrieving the gold he has thrown into the crater, Estéban refuses.

> I do not wish to tell him why I cannot accept his offer, that the burial of the gold has not absolved me of the evil nor of the wrongs I have done to myself and to others. I cannot say to him that although I am a prisoner in a fortress surrounded by the sea . . . in a cell with only one small window, still at last, at last I am free. Nor can I say to him that it is he himself who is really the prisoner, he and . . . all the rest who now dream of finding the hidden gold.[2]

The King's Fifth is one of O'Dell's best books, and Estéban de Sandoval is one of O'Dell's finest characters. The story is exciting, and the way O'Dell uses flashbacks to tell the story of the hunt for gold keeps the book full of suspense.

The King's Fifth also sends an important message about the destructiveness of greed. Estéban learns this valuable lesson, making a moral journey during the expedition. His character changes a great deal during the course of the book, and not just for the better. Literary critic Malcolm Usrey says, "The shifts in the growth and development of Estéban's insight and understanding make him a dynamic character who changes for worse, then better."[3]

In addition to winning a Newbery Honor in 1967, *The King's Fifth* won several other honors as well. O'Dell's winning streak continued with the publication of his next book, *The Black Pearl*.

The Black Pearl

Similar to *The King's Fifth*, *The Black Pearl*, published in 1967, is a story about the dangers of greed. It is a simple story that draws a clear line between good and evil.

Like the *Island of the Blue Dolphins*, *The Black Pearl* is based on a California legend O'Dell had heard. This tale, about a black pearl taken from the undersea cave of a giant manta ray, took place in the city of La Paz, Mexico. To learn more about the story and the setting, O'Dell traveled to La Paz twice.

The Black Pearl tells the story of Ramón Salazar, a young boy who discovers an enormous black pearl, which villagers call the Pearl of Heaven, while learning to dive for pearls. He discovers the pearl in an underwater cave that is rumored to be guarded by the Manta Diablo, a giant manta ray that everyone in Ramón's village fears.

Ramón is not afraid of the Manta Diablo, even though his mother has described it to him as having seven rows of teeth sharp enough to snap Ramón's bones like sticks. When the old man who is teaching Ramón to dive encourages him to throw the pearl back into the sea, Ramón refuses because he knows the pearl is valuable. The old man warns him, saying, "Someday the Manta Diablo will have [the pearl] back and your life with it. Of this I warn you."[4]

Ramón brings the pearl to his father, Blas, who is a pearl dealer. Blas tries to sell it but cannot get the price he wants. To spite the buyers who would not give him enough money for the pearl, Blas gives the pearl to the local church, where it is placed in the hands of a Madonna statue. He denies that the gift was given in spite and says that "for this gift of the great pearl [we] shall be favored in Heaven, now and forever."[5] However, rather than bringing good things, the gift of the pearl seems to bring only bad. Blas drowns, and all of his ships sink in a storm. Only one of Blas's employees—Gaspar Ruiz, known as the Sevillano—survives the storm.

Now convinced that the Pearl of Heaven is cursed, Ramón decides to throw it back into the sea, returning it to the Manta Diablo. He believes it's the only way to break the curse. However, the Sevillano, who wants the pearl for himself, tries to prevent Ramón from throwing the pearl into the ocean. He follows Ramón out to sea, where he and Ramón battle each other and fight the Manta Diablo.

The Sevillano loses the battle to the Manta Diablo and is carried away on the back of the giant beast. Ramón returns the pearl to the church, giving it back to the Madonna statue whose "hand was held out to all sinners, whoever they were, even me. In her hand I placed the great black pearl. 'This now is a gift of adoration,' I said, 'a gift of love.'"[6] Ramón then says "a prayer for the soul of the Sevillano and one for [himself]." He continues, "I also said a prayer for the Manta Diablo, that creature of beauty and of evil . . . whom everyone in this life at sometime comes to know."[7]

Ramón realizes that this unselfish gift has helped him to grow up and become a man. As O'Dell's biographer David Russell says, he has also "learned the lesson of humility in the face of nature's beautiful, but destructive, forces."[8]

The Black Pearl can be considered a fable. Although it takes place in a specific location, it could have happened at almost any time in history. It is also a bit of a mystery. Is the Manta Diablo real? Whether it is real is not important. More important is what the Manta Diablo represents: the power of nature and the evil that greed can do.

This short but powerful novel won yet another Newbery Honor. It also solidified Scott O'Dell's career as a young-adult novelist.

5 More Stories from the Past

Scott O'Dell's first three novels for young adults all took place in historical settings. He went on to write fourteen more historical novels, later mixing in contemporary novels and books for younger children.

O'Dell's fourth young adult novel, *The Dark Canoe*, was published in 1968. It was his first young adult book that was not a huge success. The story was loosely based on parts of *Moby Dick*, a novel that O'Dell loved. Although *The Dark Canoe* "contains adventure and intrigue,"[1] there is not much to the plot and most critics gave the book a negative review.

Sing Down the Moon

Sing Down the Moon was O'Dell's next award-winning work. Published in 1970, it won a 1971 Newbery Honor.

Although the story itself is fiction, it is based on an actual event: the Long Walk, in which the U.S. government forced the Navajo Indians to walk from their homes to Fort Sumner, New Mexico, in 1864. For most of the 8,000 to 9,000 Navajos, it was a 300-mile (483 km) march, and hundreds died along the way.

The story of the Long Walk is told through the eyes of a Navajo teenager named Bright Morning. She describes Navajo traditions while telling of the forced march and the hardships the Navajo suffered along the way. Like Karana in *Island of the Blue Dolphins*, Bright Morning is a strong female main character who grows a great deal over the course of the novel.

Although some critics wrote that *Sing Down the Moon* was too short and too simple to do justice to the important story of the Long Walk, others praised it for its forceful attack against the mistreatment of Native Americans at the hands of white settlers. Malcolm Usrey wrote, "O'Dell strikes at the indifference of the whites toward the suffering caused the Indians by monstrous cruelty and by not understanding the Indians' attitudes, religion, or way of life."[2]

Three More Historical Novels

In 1975, O'Dell's next historical novel, *The Hawk That Dare Not Hunt by Day*, was published. The novel takes place in Europe from 1524 to 1536, and the story is divided into five sections. It is a complex tale and is filled with interesting characters, including Tom Barton, the narrator. There is also plenty of greed and violence, although one of O'Dell's strong messages in the book is that good does sometimes win over evil.

David Russell wrote that O'Dell's "ultimate message is that we must forgive our enemies if we ourselves are to find peace of mind. This is the lesson learned by Karana and a host of other O'Dell protagonists."[3]

Critics, including Malcolm Usrey, praised *The Hawk That Dare Not Hunt by Day*. Usrey said that the book "is as good as any historical novel O'Dell has written. It has a gripping plot, the characterization is well done, especially that of Tom Barton, and it is a highly accurate recounting of the political and religious turmoil and strife surrounding the beginnings of the Reformation in England."[4]

The 290, a novel set during the Civil War (1861–1865), was published in 1976. The story is told from the point of view of a sixteen-year-old named Jim Lynne, a Southerner whose father is a wealthy slave trader. Jim, who ran away from home a few years before, sails on the *290*, a British warship that is helping the Confederacy in the Civil War.

Jim's adventures take him to Haiti, to England, and then back home to America. Although *The 290* is full of historical facts and details, many critics wrote that it was too rambling and disconnected to be a good story.

Another O'Dell historical novel about war was published in 1977. *Carlota* is narrated by a young woman living in California during the Mexican-American War. Carlota's character is loosely based on a real woman, Luisa Montero. Unlike many of his other books, *Carlota* focuses on the characters rather than on the plot. Some critics praised O'Dell for this aspect of the novel, but others wrote that it hurt the story, which they said went on for too long.

A Sequel, of Sorts

After *Island of the Blue Dolphins* was published, many readers wrote to O'Dell begging to know what had happened to Karana after she left the island. Years later, with letters still arriving, O'Dell decided to write about Karana again. However, he did not want to write a direct sequel to *Island of the Blue Dolphins*. Instead, he wrote *Zia*, which was published in 1976.

Zia is a story told from the point of view of Zia, Karana's niece, who has grown up on the mainland. Zia and her brother, Mando, live at the Santa Barbara Mission and dream of rescuing their aunt. Together, they try to get to the island to save Karana, but their rescue attempts are unsuccessful.

When Karana is eventually brought to the mission, she is unable to speak the language of any of the Native Americans living there, so Zia and Mando aren't able to learn about her adventures on the island. Karana dies not long after coming to the mission.

Shortly before it was published, O'Dell said that he believed *Zia* would "be compared, and I think unfavorably, with *Island of the Blue Dolphins*. That's inevitable; however, I think this book stands on its own."[5]

Zia's story is an interesting one, and she is a strong character, like her aunt. However, many readers were disappointed with *Zia* because they didn't learn anything about what Karana was thinking or feeling after her rescue and during her short time living at the mission.

The Seven Serpents Trilogy

In the late 1970s, O'Dell began working on *The Captive*, the first book in what would become a trilogy. The three books in the Seven Serpents trilogy—*The Captive* (1979), *The Feathered Serpent* (1981), and *The Amethyst Ring* (1983)—are about the ancient Mayan, Aztec, and Incan civilizations. O'Dell was very interested in all three early cultures and went to Central and South America at least three times to do research for these books. His extensive research is evident in his vivid descriptions of the locations and in the details he provides.

The Captive introduces Julián Escobar, the main character in all three books. Through his adventures, readers learn many facts about Mayan culture and plenty of historical information. Julián's adventures are exciting, as well as informative, and *The Captive* ends with a cliff-hanger, leaving readers uncertain about where Julián's adventures will take him.

Two years later, readers were able to find out what happens to Julián. The next book in the trilogy, *The Feathered Serpent*, picks up where *The*

Captive left off. In this second book, we learn about the Aztec civilization as we follow Julián on his further adventures. *The Amethyst Ring* continues Julián's story and concludes the trilogy. This time Julián's travels bring him in contact with the Incas.

Although all of the books in the trilogy are exciting and fast-paced, some critics say that none of them allows readers to get to know some of the characters well. Even Julián, who appears in all three books is, according to David Russell, "thinly drawn . . . with unconvincing motivation and virtually nonexistent emotions."[6]

Another criticism of the books in the Seven Serpents trilogy is that the stories are not always believable. In addition, the reader who already knows a little about any of the three ancient civilizations "knows the civilizations will fall, and how and why," according to Malcolm Usrey. "But, from O'Dell's trilogy, the reader does not know how it felt to be either the conquerors or the conquered."[7]

A New Home Inspires a New Book

In 1979, Scott O'Dell and his wife, Elizabeth Hall, moved to Westchester County, New York, just north of New York City. O'Dell had lived most of his life in Southern California, but he welcomed the change of scenery.

Always interested in local legends, O'Dell researched historical stories about his new neighborhood. He heard about a woman named Sarah Bishop, who had lived in a cave in the late 1700s, in Westchester County. O'Dell grew interested in her story and wondered why she had retreated from her community. He began doing research on her but said "the only information was one short paragraph about her in a newspaper of the time she died. I took that sparse information and created Sarah Bishop. I put fiction and fact together to create her. Sarah Bishop lives through me and my words."[8]

In the version of her life O'Dell created in *Sarah Bishop* (1980), we learn that Sarah is torn between her father and brother, who are on opposite sides in the Revolutionary War (1775–1783). Sarah's father is loyal to England, and her brother supports the rebels. When both her father and brother die, Sarah is on her own. Sarah endures some traumatic events and eventually decides to make a home for herself in a cave. Much like Karana in *Island of the Blue Dolphins*, Sarah must learn to survive in a harsh environment with little or no help from others. The townspeople find Sarah strange and accuse her of witchcraft, although she is later acquitted. Near the end of the book, Sarah begins to take small steps toward rejoining the community.

Sarah is yet another resilient female character created by O'Dell. Unlike in some other books O'Dell wrote, readers really get to know the heroine—what she is thinking and feeling. Another strength of *Sarah Bishop* is that it shows both sides of the Revolutionary War, rather than featuring only one point of view.

Another String of Historical Novels

After *Sarah Bishop* and the Seven Serpents trilogy, O'Dell turned to European history. His book *Road to Damietta*, about St. Francis of Assisi, was published in 1985. St. Francis's life story is told through the eyes of a girl named Ricca, who is in love with him. Ricca is thirteen when the book begins, and their story unfolds over the next twenty years. Some reviewers said this was one of O'Dell's best books, but others criticized him for focusing the story on Ricca. They wrote that O'Dell did not provide enough information about St. Francis and what he thought or felt.

To research his next book, *Streams to the River, River to the Sea: A Novel of Sacagawea* (1986), O'Dell "followed—by car, foot, and boat—Sacagawea's long trail through the Rocky Mountains,"[9] according to interviewer Lee Bennett Hopkins. Sacagawea was the Native American woman who accompanied explorers Meriwether Lewis and William Clark part way on their expedition to explore the American West from 1804 to 1806. Journeying from the mouth of the Missouri River to the Pacific Ocean and back, the group mapped the land, studied plants and animals, and took notes on the people they encountered along the way.

Sacagawea, along with her husband and their baby (who was born during the trip) is one of the most famous Native Americans. David Russell wrote that in his portrayal of Sacagawea, "O'Dell has given us a flesh-and-blood heroine who endures real physical and spiritual hardships."[10]

Streams to the River, River to the Sea also shows O'Dell's deep respect for nature and the strong connection Native Americans had with the natural world. The closing lines of the novel illustrate this respect:

> In the morning we were on the trail at sunrise. The sky was deep blue and cloudless. Locusts sang in the high grass. The wild blooms of summer were everywhere. I picked a handful for [my son].

He laughed and smelled them. One day when he was older I would tell him that the wild blooms were the footprints of little children, those who had gone away and come back to gladden us. I would tell him many things that the Shoshone people knew.[11]

O'Dell's next book also focused on a Native American woman. *The Serpent Never Sleeps: A Novel of Jamestown and Pocahontas* (1987) tells the story of Pocahontas from the time of her capture by the English until her death. Serena Lynn, a young English servant of a slave trader who has sailed to Plymouth colony with the slave trader's son, narrates the story. The book is filled with details about life in England, as well as life in the early days of America.

My Name Is Not Angelica (1989) was O'Dell's next historical novel. The story of a slave revolt in 1753, it is narrated by Raisha, a young girl who is taken from her home in Africa and made a slave on the Caribbean island of St. John. *My Name Is Not Angelica* was the last book O'Dell published before his death in 1989.

6 Some New Approaches

Although Scott O'Dell is best known for his books about topics taken from history, he wrote several other types of books for young adults and children. His first attempt at a new type of book was with *Journey to Jericho*, a story for elementary-school children.

Books for Younger Readers

Journey to Jericho was a new type of book for O'Dell in two ways: it was set in the present day; and it was written for young children, as opposed to young adults and adults, who were the audience of his previous books.

Published in 1969, *Journey to Jericho* is about David, a nine-year-old boy traveling from

West Virginia to California with his family to meet his father, who has gone ahead to find a job. The story begins with details about the coal-mining town where David lived in West Virginia. These details were drawn from an experience O'Dell had when he visited relatives in West Virginia when he was young.

> The miners with lamps on their caps, the blind mules that shoved the carts back and forth in the mine, and the small steam engine that pulled it away to the railroad tipple—all these things fascinated me. Remembering them and that long-ago summer, I wrote *Journey to Jericho*.[1]

A few years after *Journey to Jericho* was published, O'Dell wrote another book for young children. *The Treasure of Topo-el-Bampo* (1972) is based on a Mexican folktale from the 1700s. It tells the tale of a very poor village and focuses on a favorite O'Dell theme: the power and dangers of greed.

A Sea Voyage Becomes a Book

Scott O'Dell loved to travel. "Travel to me is more important than anything,"[2] he told interviewer Lee Bennett Hopkins. Before writing many of his books, he would visit the locations where he planned for them to take place. He said, "I always visit a place I am going to write about. That gives me the true feeling of the locale, the weather, the land, the sky, the people who once lived there."[3] One of his trips, taken in the early 1970s, became *The Cruise of the Arctic Star* (1973). The book recounts O'Dell's trip up the West Coast from San Diego to the Columbia River. His wife went along and served as navigator. A friend and a man hired to help them sail the 50-foot (15 m) boat also came along for the trip.

The Cruise of the Arctic Star combines many of O'Dell's interests. In it he wrote about California history, sailing and navigation, and the importance of preserving the environment and the plants and animals in it. He recounted stories from his own personal history and years of living in California. O'Dell also discussed the many early explorers who sailed along the Pacific Coast. In the introduction to the book, O'Dell wrote:

> Much of the story is a voyage into the past. It follows in the wake of the Spanish explorers Juan Cabrillo and Sebastián Vizcaíno, the English pirate Sir Francis Drake, the merchant sailor Richard Henry Dana and captains of the New England clippers. It also follows the footsteps of such landsmen as Father Serra, Jed Smith, Lean John, Kit Carson and John Sutter.

So the book has to do with the land and the sea, the past and the present.[4]

Problem Novels

In the 1970s, many books written for young adult readers told the stories of teens facing serious problems such as pregnancy, drug use, and rape. These novels were called problem novels. Scott O'Dell wrote two problem novels: *Child of Fire* (1974) and *Kathleen, Please Come Home* (1978).

Child of Fire is the story of Manuel, a Hispanic teenage gang member who gets into trouble several times and ends up in jail in South America. However, by the end of the book, he becomes a hero when he is killed at a worker protest at a local vineyard. According to critics, the main problem with this book is that it is told from the point of view of Manuel's parole officer. This makes it difficult to know what Manuel is thinking and feeling during his misadventures. David Russell said that it was an "inaccurate and condescending portrayal of Hispanic culture."[5]

Several years later, O'Dell wrote another problem novel, this time featuring a teenage runaway who is pregnant and involved with drugs. *Kathleen, Please Come Home* is written in an interesting way. It is divided into three parts and is written to resemble diary entries. The first and last parts are the diary entries of Kathleen. The middle part consists of Kathleen's mother's diary entries. Although this is a fast-paced book and deals with serious issues, parts of it are not very believable.

Contemporary Stories

Several of the books O'Dell wrote in the mid- to late 1980s feature contemporary female characters in interesting situations. *The Spanish Smile* (1982) and its sequel, *The Castle in the Sea* (1983), tell the story of a rich family living on an island off the coast of California.

In *The Spanish Smile*, readers quickly realize that the father is crazy and is keeping his family as prisoners on the island. Lucinda, the daughter, who narrates the story, does not seem to realize that her father is crazy. Both of the books in this short series are similar to soap operas, with entertaining but over-the-top situations.

Alexandra (1984), O'Dell's next novel set in contemporary times, tells the story of a Greek American teenage girl living on the Gulf Coast of Florida. When Alexandra's father dies on the job in a sponge-diving accident, Alexandra learns to become a sponge diver so she can take over the family business. She discovers that workers on the family's boat, along with her older sister's fiancé, are hiding cocaine in the sponges. Alexandra must decide whether to turn the workers over to the authorities, and by the end of the book, she decides to do so. However, the book ends before we learn the outcome of her actions.

As in many of O'Dell's books, one of the main messages is that the desire to have money or other riches can corrupt people. Alexandra struggles with whether to do the right thing by turning her sister's fiancé in to the police at the risk of hurting her sister in the process. Malcolm Usrey wrote that Alexandra shows that:

> Making a moral decision may result in hardships and suffering for all involved, including the person who must make the right decision, but, because Alexandra is always an upright and honest young woman, her dilemma does not engage a reader to the degree that Estéban's does when he determines in *The King's Fifth* to throw the gold into a sulphur pit and put behind the evil person it has made him.[6]

O'Dell's last novel set in contemporary times is *Black Star, Bright Dawn*, which is about the Iditarod, the famous 1,000-mile (1,609 km) dogsled race in Alaska. To help in his preparation for writing this book, O'Dell told Lee Bennett Hopkins that he attended the races at Saranac Lake, New York. He also said:

> I own a blue-eyed Siberian husky, named "Black Star." I bought her with the thought of acquainting myself with this extraordinary breed. She is a medium-sized dog, but she can pull me off my feet. I take her in the car so if we break down she can pull us into a garage.[7]

Black Star, Bright Dawn (1988) is, as David Russell put it:

> one of O'Dell's most successful pieces of contemporary fiction—it is fast-paced with characters we care about and scenes we will remember. It is also closest in spirit to his best historical fiction, steeped as it is in local culture, grounded in a serious theme, and focused on a humble, but noble, character who has something at stake.[8]

Black Star, Bright Dawn tells the story of Bright Dawn, an Eskimo girl living in Alaska. She takes over for her father when he has to drop out of the Iditarod. Bright Dawn trains her dog team, led by Bright Star, her favorite dog, and she and her dog team work hard to prepare for the race.

During the long race, Bright Dawn overcomes many obstacles and dangerous situations. She also takes time to help others participating in the race, even when it means that she will not be able to win. For her efforts, she receives the sportsman-ship award of $2,500. At the finish of the race, when Bright Dawn receives her award, she says, "I felt richer than I ever thought I would be . . . I was happy about myself. I was not the same person who had left Ikuma long weeks ago. How I was dif-ferent, I didn't know. But it was there, deep inside me."[9] Like many of O'Dell's characters, Bright Dawn makes a journey and in the process gains maturity and wisdom.

7 A Writer and His Audience

Scott O'Dell loved to write, but writing did not come easily for him. He told Lee Bennett Hopkins that "writing is hard, harder than digging a ditch, and it requires patience. The hardest part is to sit down at an empty desk, pick up a pen, face a blank page, and write the first sentence."[1]

Along with traveling to the places he intended to use as his settings, O'Dell enjoyed doing additional research for his books. Usually, he would spend up to four months reading books and studying other sources before he began writing. If the subject he planned to write about was based on history, he would read whatever he could find about the event or the person. If not, he would read about other subjects relevant to the book, such as sponge diving for *Alexandra* or dogsled racing for *Black Star, Bright Dawn*. O'Dell always wanted his books to be as accurate and detailed as possible.

Once he had completed his research, O'Dell would sit down to write. As much as he loved to do research, the story itself was more important to O'Dell than using exact facts or details. So, during the writing phase, he also took great pains to develop the plot and consider the message he wanted the book to convey.

Each book required about six months of writing to complete. O'Dell wrote his books in several places in Europe and in Mexico. Most of the time, however, he wrote at home. When writing, O'Dell did little else. He didn't leave the house often or socialize with friends. He would write from about 5:00 AM until about noon. Some days he would go out to lunch with his wife and over lunch they would discuss what he had written that morning.

For most of his life as a writer, O'Dell used a type-writer—personal computers were not available at the time. However, when he quit smoking, he began to write his novels by hand on yellow legal pads. He had gotten so used to smoking while he typed that he had to stop typing in order to quit smoking.

To find ideas for his novels, O'Dell often began with subjects he was interested in. However, his inspiration came from many other places as well. He once said, "The writer collects from his own life and the lives of others, from the past and the present, from books, and from circumstances, those things that, in texture and tone and meaning, are appropriate to his design."[2]

Encouraging Other Writers

When asked what young adults should do to prepare for a career in writing, O'Dell had this advice:

> . . . read a lot. We learn to write by imitation. I think young people interested in writing should select a favorite author and read his or her books for pure pleasure. Ask such questions as why the author used the title, why the author opens the story at a particular point, how characters are introduced and developed, how they are described, how the author builds suspense, pace. Analyze the whole from beginning to end.
>
> Then, using your own material, try to write a book of your own. You will find that you develop your own style, your own voice, as you learn to build a story.[3]

O'Dell encouraged young people to become writers in other ways as well, and he also hoped to persuade adult authors to write more historical fiction for children. To help in this goal, he established the Scott O'Dell Award for Historical Fiction in 1982. The Scott O'Dell Award Web site says that O'Dell established the award "to increase the interest of young readers in the historical background that has helped to shape their country and their world."[4]

This award is given each year to a book for children or young adults that is a work of fiction set in Canada, the United States, or Central or South America. The book must be written in English, and the author must be a U.S. citizen. A committee of librarians and other children's book experts chooses the award recipient.

Authors of the winning books are given a $5,000 prize. Past authors include Patricia MacLachlan for *Sarah, Plain and Tall* (1986); Katherine Paterson for *Jip, His Story* (1997); and Richard Peck for *A River Between Us* (2004). Scott O'Dell accepted the award himself in 1987 for *Streams to the River, River to the Sea*.

O'Dell's Audience Responds

O'Dell didn't originally set out to be a writer of fiction for young adults, and he didn't always consider his books children's books. "Books of mine which are classified officially as books for children were not written for children," O'Dell said. "Instead, and in a very real sense, they were written for myself."[5]

However, O'Dell very much enjoyed writing for young adults. He said, "Of all the audiences, children are the finest."[6] He loved getting feedback from readers and received as many as 2,000 letters from them every year. He was gratified to hear from them, explaining that children sent "thousands of letters, over an indefinite period of time." He continued, "It is this response and concern that to me make the work of an author worth doing."[7]

With his books, O'Dell said he wanted to:

. . . teach and say something to people. Adults have pretty well established their lives, but you can say something to children. If you can get their attention and affection, then there is something that can really be done with children. You can tell a story and add something that might be of interest and importance in their lives.[8]

O'Dell also wanted to help children understand that even though they may have problems, they are not alone. He explained:

It is good for children to think that they are unique, as different from one another as are their thumb prints. But it is not good for them to think that their problems are unique. People before them had problems to solve—many of the same problems, or related ones, by which children are now bedeviled.[9]

8 A Long and Successful Career Comes to an End

O'Dell never stopped writing. He did take time out to travel and enjoy the world around him, but he continued to write and publish novels for young readers right until his death.

Throughout the 1980s, O'Dell and his wife lived in a house on a lake in Westchester County, New York. When he wasn't writing, he spent time gardening, watching the local wildlife, and reading in the sun. O'Dell describes the setting:

> My house is on the shore of a lake, surrounded by a forest of oak and maple and birch, where geese glide on the water, cardinals breakfast beside us, raccoons call each

night for dinner, and deer dine on our shrubs . . . All this wildlife keeps my dog, a Siberian husky who roams through the pages of *Black Star, Bright Dawn*, in a continual state of excitement.[1]

Dolphins Honor O'Dell

Scott O'Dell died on October 15, 1989, of prostate cancer. He was ninety-one years old and had lived a life full of great accomplishments. His twenty-six books for children and young adults won numerous awards, and children and adults alike appreciated his exciting and moving novels.

Several months after he died, O'Dell's family brought his ashes out on a boat as they sailed off the coast of Southern California. They scattered his ashes into the Pacific Ocean and celebrated O'Dell's life. When they turned the boat around and headed back toward shore, ten or twelve dolphins began swimming next to the boat, leaping alongside it. The dolphins accompanied the boat all the way back to the entrance to the harbor in San Diego. It was a fitting tribute to a man who had loved and honored dolphins and other creatures in his life and work.

A Postscript

O'Dell left two books unfinished upon his death. Shortly before he died, he had been working on a book about Chief Joseph of the Nez Percé Indians. His wife, Elizabeth Hall, who is also a writer, finished the book, which was published in 1992. Titled *Thunder Rolling in the Mountains*, the story is told by Chief Joseph's fourteen-year-old daughter, Sound of Running Feet. There is a great deal of death and violence in the book, but it is true to the real story of Chief Joseph.

O'Dell had also begun researching a book about dolphins before he died. He had not completed work on it, but Elizabeth Hall used some of his research to write *Venus Among the Fishes* (1995), which is about the capture of a dolphin and the dolphin's subsequent adventures as a marine show performer.

O'Dell's Message to Readers

O'Dell's work has much to teach us. Many of his books emphasize the importance of preserving our natural environment and the creatures in it. He also used his books to send a strong message of tolerance for people of all races, religions, and ideas.

O'Dell always remembered the importance of getting his message to young people everywhere, saying:

> It is very rewarding for me to write for children. I have a sincere feeling that I am able to say something to children, that someone is listening. I am

not just entertaining them; I hope that somewhere in each of my books there is something they will take away from it that is important to them as a person.[2]

Most important of all to O'Dell was this: "With all of my books, I've tried to dramatize the importance of the dignity of the human spirit. That has been my goal, and everything I have written has been with that in mind."[3] Readers of O'Dell's work would agree that in this goal, O'Dell succeeded.

Interview with Scott O'Dell

Excerpted from *The Pied Pipers: Interviews with the Influential Creators of Children's Literature* by Justin Wintle and Emma Fisher.

JUSTIN WINTLE: Many of your books . . . are concerned with traditional American themes, particularly themes of the frontier—conquest of new lands, what it's like to be midway between having laws made for you and making them for yourself, the conflict of interests between the old tribes and the new settlers, and the sense of opportunity given to youth. Is this because of the life you've led?

SCOTT O'DELL: I've been asked that question before, and I've never given what I thought was an adequate answer. I've led a very full life, gone to many schools, done a lot of things, lived abroad extensively, been in a couple of wars. A mixed up sort of life, perhaps. I think the fact that I've written about the past has to do with this. It's not necessarily an escape (though I think there's part of that in it), or an attempt to look back at calmer times; rather I have the feeling that the present is the past and the past is the present. The fundamental human is about the same as he was a couple of thousand years ago. The basic changes have not been vast. Human needs for love, affection, understanding, a chance to succeed at something, are about the same. Although I may write about a Navajo girl (*Sing Down the Moon*), I feel that she is a contemporary. I just wanted to pay a tribute to the human spirit, and the fact that this spirit happened to be in an Indian girl is really incidental.

JUSTIN WINTLE: [*Island of the Blue Dolphins*] is another book that has an Indian girl as its heroine. Why is it that you write so sympathetically about the Indians?

SCOTT O'DELL: I think it is accidental, in the sense that I've lived in a country of Indians. The story of an Indian girl who lives eighteen years on an island alone is a dramatic idea, so I used it as a vehicle for what I wanted to say. If she had been a girl from Iowa or the *Mayflower* I still would have done it, because of the situation. The same with the Navajo girl in *Sing Down the Moon*, a ready-made situation about a people who were persecuted, uprooted and driven from their homes . . . I think of all this as just an accident, that I was born out here. If I'd been born in the Middle West and stayed in the Middle West, I would come into contact with different legends, probably about early French voyages and so forth.

JUSTIN WINTLE: Your books are all told in the first person, through the eyes of the protagonist. Is that because many of them are based on stories you've heard word of mouth?

SCOTT O'DELL: I think it's the easiest way to write, though some of my adult books have been written in the third person . . . I think writing in the third person is easier because you don't have to work so hard for suspension of disbelief. When you read that "I did it" there's a tendency to believe what you're being told. You get an almost automatic identification which I think is so important in a story.

JUSTIN WINTLE: Are your books intended as a way through the barriers between children and their parents?

SCOTT O'DELL: Yes—I think the written word is one of the few great resources we have. I don't think our television, with its violence . . . is helpful at all. I have a dedication to the idea of trying to reach this young group that hasn't been abandoned yet, to reach them with a few simple comments about life. I get a lot of letters from children, particularly on *Island of the Blue Dolphins*. They like the idea of fighting for survival; they are challenged by it and they would like to try it themselves.

Timeline

1898 Odell Gabriel Scott (Scott O'Dell) is born in Los Angeles, California, on May 23.

1918 O'Dell joins the U.S. Army and attends training at Occidental College in California. He is released from the army on December 17, 1918.

1920 O'Dell attends the University of Wisconsin. He then enrolls at Stanford University.

Early 1920s O'Dell evaluates photoplays for the Palmer Photoplay Company. He changes his name to Scott O'Dell after a newspaper error reverses his names.

1924 *Representative Photoplays Analyzed*, O'Dell's first book, is published while he works for the Paramount Motion Picture Studio in Hollywood, California.

1925 O'Dell works on the film crew of *Ben Hur* in Rome, Italy. He attends the University of Rome and writes his first novel, *Pinfeathers*. It is never published.

1927 O'Dell returns to the United States.

1934 *Woman of Spain: A Story of California* is published.

1947 O'Dell begins working as a book reviewer at the *Los Angeles Daily News*.

1960 *Island of the Blue Dolphins*, O'Dell's first novel for young adults, is published.

1961 O'Dell receives the Newbery Medal (and several other awards) for *Island of the Blue Dolphins*.

1967 *The King's Fifth* receives a Newbery Honor.

1968 *The Black Pearl* receives a Newbery Honor.

1971 *Sing Down the Moon* receives a Newbery Honor.

1972 O'Dell receives the Hans Christian Andersen Award.

1976 O'Dell receives the University of Southern Mississippi Award.

1978 O'Dell receives the Catholic Library Association Regina Medal.

1982 The Scott O'Dell Award for Historical Fiction is established.

1989 O'Dell receives the Children's Literature Award from School Media Specialists of Southeastern New York. O'Dell receives the Northern Westchester Center for the Arts Award. He dies on October 15 in Mt. Kisco, New York.

Selected Reviews from *School Library Journal*

The Black Pearl
December 1967

Gr 7–10—Off the coast of Baja California, 16-year-old Ramon Salazar confronts his two enemies—the Manta Diablo, a monster devilfish with a fabled reputation, and the unscrupulous Ruiz, the finest pearl diver in his father's fleet. From the encounter, Ramon learns that possession of the magnificent 60-carat black pearl which he had found and his father had given to the local church is no simple matter. Depending on his munificent gift of the pearl to the Madonna to earn the protection of Heaven, the elder Salazar took the fleet out in a severe storm, and all except the cynical Ruiz were lost.

Ramon determines to return the pearl to the sea but must first battle both Ruiz and that manta. Subtly revealed throughout is the idea that personal sacrifice is required to achieve a great ambition and that a gift to heaven does not cancel the need for either common sense or self-reliance. Spare, distinguished writing elucidates these timeless, universal themes in a contemporary setting.

The Captive
October 1979

Gr 7–12—A superbly written novel, rich in plot and historical detail, that explores Spanish penetration in the Americas in the early 16th Century. A follower of Bartolomé de las Casas, an anti-slavery priest, 16-year-old Julián Escobar is yanked from his studies at the seminary in Seville for a journey to the island of Buanaaventura in the New World. When the ship lands and the Spaniards discover gold, Julián witnesses acts of brutality against the peaceful inhabitants that sicken him and is afraid to speak out. A hurricane sinks the ship and Julian believes he and the horse Bravo are the only survivors on an uninhabited island. He leads a Robinson Crusoe existence until he finds a hideous idol, from which he deduces there must be others nearby. Ceela, a young Mayan girl, leaves him fire and food and, in exchange for rides on Bravo, teaches him her language and customs and tells him about the great city of the Seven Serpents. She is uninterested in Christianity and, with some explosives salvaged from the ship, he blows up the idol. The next day, he is visited by a delegation from the City led by a Spaniard, a crafty dwarf named Guillermo Cantu, who tells Julián the Mayan legend of the god Kukulcán: how he disappeared and promised to return as a young, blond man. Despite himself, Julián is dawn into Cantu's plot to pass him off as the god. The book—"the first part of a story to be called City of the Seven Serpents," according to an author's note—ends with Julián, standing atop a pyramid, accepted as Kukulcán and already seduced by the glory that will be his. Characterizations are all finely dawn, and Julián's transformation from insecure, humane seminarian to pretend god is remarkable in its honest development.

The King's Fifth
February 1967

Gr 7–9—While awaiting trial for murder and withholding from the king the obligatory fifth of the gold found in Cîbola, Estéban, a 17-year-old map-maker, recalls his hardships and adventures on an expedition to the famed cities. Led by the gold-hungry Captain Mendoza of Coronado's army and guided by an Indian girl, the party of seven pushed their way across mountains and conquered Indian villages to get the precious metal—with dire results. Eventually Estéban, in sole possession of the treasure, is faced with a decision of moral survival and chooses to throw the gold into the sulphurous waters of a desert crater. An especially effective narrative technique enhances the suspense: Estéban's descriptions of the past are interspersed with chapters on the progress of the trial, so that we can see him at once in prison and on his journey. Motivations and characterizations are finely drawn, and ethical values are implicit in this excellent novel of the 16th century which brings to life people and events.

Sarah Bishop
May 1980

Gr 6 Up—Sarah Bishop's home in New York is destroyed during the Revolution when her Loyalist father dies after being tarred and feathered. Searching for her brother, she is mistakenly accused by the British of setting a fire and makes a daring escape to Westchester County. Settling by a lake, with only an ax and jackknife, Sarah begins to make a life for herself. Her ability to survive—gathering food, fending off the unwelcome visit of a trapper, accepting the help of an Indian couple, recovering from a copperhead bite, even standing trial at the nearest village as a witch—becomes her source of strength and comfort; she faces danger and obstacles with an unusual but believable combination of determination and courage. Her isolation from others takes its spiritual toll, however, and it is only through her friendship with the Quaker Isaac Morton that her faith begins to revive. There are few heroes in this story. The harsh life of the settlers is well portrayed and the historical background (not just Tory vs. Patriot) is well integrated. Readers will especially relish Sarah's fierce independence; her triumph over personal tragedy and adversity makes for memorable reading, and her adventures in the wilderness provide a dramatic setting.

Zia
March 1976

Gr 4–7—Fourteen-year-old Zia's goal to rescue her aunt, Karana, marooned for many years in *Island of the Blue Dolphins* (Houghton, 1960), seems closer when she and her brother find a storm-beached whaleboat and try to row to the island.

They fail but Captain Nidever promises to get Karana when he hunts otter there. When he returns with Karana, no one at the mission, including Zia, can speak Karana's dialect. Karana, though happy, finds it hard to accept the regimented life at the mission and moves into a cave. In spite of Zia's love and care, Karana sickens and dies and Zia, free of ties, leaves for her own home with Karana's dog. In comparison to *Island* . . . this seems almost a postscript or second ending (it changes O'Dell's statement that Karana found none of her people on the mainland), but Zia is an excellent story in its own right, written in a clear, quiet, and reflective style which is in harmony with the plot and characterization. While not action filled, readers are drawn compellingly on, and there are some beautifully vivid word pictures and a reasonable amount of background information on 18th century California Mission life well integrated.

List of
Selected Works

Alexandra. Boston, MA: Houghton Mifflin Company, 1984.

The Amethyst Ring. Boston, MA: Houghton Mifflin Company, 1983.

The Black Pearl. Boston, MA: Houghton Mifflin Company, 1967.

Black Star, Bright Dawn. Boston, MA: Houghton Mifflin Company, 1988.

The Captive. Boston, MA: Houghton Mifflin Company, 1979.

Carlota. Boston, MA: Houghton Mifflin Company, 1977.

Child of Fire. Boston, MA: Houghton Mifflin Company, 1974.

The Cruise of the Arctic Star. Boston, MA: Houghton Mifflin Company, 1973.

The Dark Canoe. Boston, MA: Houghton Mifflin Company, 1968.

The Feathered Serpent. Boston, MA: Houghton Mifflin Company, 1981.

The Hawk That Dare Not Hunt by Day. Boston, MA: Houghton Mifflin Company, 1975.

Island of the Blue Dolphins. Boston, MA: Houghton Mifflin Company, 1960.

Journey to Jericho. Boston, MA: Houghton Mifflin Company, 1969.

Kathleen, Please Come Home. Boston, MA: Houghton Mifflin Company, 1978.

The King's Fifth. Boston, MA: Houghton Mifflin Company, 1966.

My Name Is Not Angelica. Boston, MA: Houghton Mifflin Company, 1989.

The Road to Damietta. Boston, MA: Houghton Mifflin Company, 1985.

Sarah Bishop. Boston, MA: Houghton Mifflin Company, 1980.

The Serpent Never Sleeps: A Novel of Jamestown and Pocahontas. Boston, MA: Houghton Mifflin Company, 1987.

Sing Down the Moon. Boston, MA: Houghton Mifflin Company, 1970.

The Spanish Smile. Boston, MA: Houghton Mifflin Company, 1982.

Streams to the River, River to the Sea: A Novel of Sacagawea. Boston, MA: Houghton Mifflin Company, 1986.

Thunder Rolling in the Mountains, with Elizabeth Hall. Boston, MA: Houghton Mifflin Company, 1992.

The Treasure of Topo-el-Bampo. Boston, MA: Houghton Mifflin Company, 1972.

The 290. Boston, MA: Houghton Mifflin Company, 1976.

Zia. Boston, MA: Houghton Mifflin Company, 1976.

List of
Selected Awards

FOCAL Award, Los Angeles Public Library, 1981, for "excellence in creative work that enriches a child's understanding of California"

Hans Christian Andersen Medal for lifetime achievement, 1972

Northern Westchester Center for the Arts Award, 1989

Regina Medal, Catholic Library Association, 1978, for body of work

School Library Media Specialist of Southeastern New York Award for contribution to children's literature, 1989

University of Southern Mississippi Medallion, 1976

Alexandra **(1984)**
Parents' Choice Award for Literature, Parents
 Choice Foundation, 1984

The Black Pearl **(1967)**
ALA Notable Book citation, 1968
Horn Book honor citation, 1968
Newbery Honor Book, 1968

Black Star, Bright Dawn **(1988)**
Woodward Park Book Award, 1989

Child of Fire **(1974)**
ALA Notable Book citation, 1974
Children's Book of the Year citation, Child
 Study Association of America, 1974
New York Times Outstanding Book citation, 1974

The Hawk That Dare Not Hunt by Day **(1975)**
Children's Book of the Year citation, Child Study
 Association of America, 1975

Island of the Blue Dolphins **(1960)**
ALA Notable Book citation, 1985
German Juvenile International Award, 1963
Hans Christian Andersen Award of Merit, Inter-
 national Board on Books for Young People, 1962

Lewis Carroll Shelf Award, 1961
Nene Award, Hawaii Library Association, 1964
Newbery Medal, 1961
OMAR Award, 1985
Pomora Friends of the Library Award, 1961
Rupert Hughes Award, 1960
Southern California Council on Literature for
    Children and Young People Notable Book
    Award, 1961
William Allen White Award, 1963

The King's Fifth (1966)
German Juvenile International Award, 1968
Horn Book honor citation, 1967
Newbery Honor Book, 1967

Sing Down the Moon (1970)
ALA Notable Book citation, 1971
Children's Book of the Year citation, Child Study
    Association of America, 1970
Freedoms Foundation Award, 1973
Horn Book honor citation, 1971
Newbery Honor Book, 1971

Streams to the River, River to the Sea:
A Novel of Sacagawea (1986)
Children's Book of the Year citation, Child Study
    Association of America, 1987

Parents' Choice Award for Literature, Parents
   Choice Foundation, 1986
Scott O'Dell Award for Historical Fiction, 1986

The Treasure of Topo-el-Bampo **(1972)**
Children's Book of the Year citation, Child Study
   Association of America, 1972

The 290 **(1976)**
Children's Book of the Year citation, Child Study
   Association of America, 1976

Zia **(1976)**
ALA Notable Book citation
Children's Book of the Year citation, Child Study
   Association of America, 1976

Glossary

Aleut A person from a string of volcanic islands near Alaska.

avid Enthusiastic or eager.

biographer A person who writes a history of someone else's life.

breakwater A wall that protects a harbor from the large waves of the open ocean.

complacency Calm or satisfaction.

devilfish A giant manta ray.

fable A short, fictitious story intended to teach a lesson.

genre A particular type or category of music, art, or literature.

manta ray A large, flat fish usually found in warm water, also known as a devilfish.

née Formerly known as.

pinfeather A feather that is not fully developed.

protagonist The main character in a novel.

prow The front of a ship or boat.

remonstrate To present and urge reasons in opposition.

resilient Able to recover from or adjust to misfortune or change.

sandspit A small strip of land that juts out into the water.

stagnate To be inactive.

stolid Expressing little feeling.

sulphur A natural element that usually exists in the form of yellow crystals but can be dissolved in water.

tipple The place where cars loaded with coal are emptied.

trilogy A series of three books that are connected and usually share a similar theme.

trinket Small piece of jewelry that is of little value.

typeset To prepare written material to be printed.

For More Information

American Library Association
50 East Huron Street
Chicago, IL 60611-2795
(800) 545-2433
Web site: http://www.ala.org

High School Teachers @ Random House, Inc.
Random House, Inc.
Children's Books
1745 Broadway
New York, NY 10019
e-mail: highschool@randomhouse.com
Web site: http://www.randomhouse.com/
   highschool/authors/odell.html

The Newbery Medal Home Page
Association for Library Service to Children
American Library Association
50 East Huron St.
Chicago, IL 60611-2795
(800) 545-2433 ext. 2163
e-mail: alsc@ala.org
Web site: http://www.ala.org/ala/alsc/
   awardsscholarships/literaryawds/
   newberymedal/newberymedal.htm

Web Sites

Due to the changing nature of Internet links, The
Rosen Publishing Group, Inc., has developed an
online list of Web sites related to the subject of
this book. This site is updated regularly. Please
use this link to access the list:

http://www.rosenlinks.com/lab/sode

For Further Reading

Bostrom, Kathleen Long. *Winning Authors: Profiles of Newbery Medalists.* Westport, CT: Libraries Unlimited, 2003.

Commire, Anne, ed. *Something About the Author: Facts and Pictures About Contemporary Authors and Illustrators of Books for Young People.* Vol. 134. Detroit, MI: Gale Group, Inc., 2003.

Gallo, Donald R., ed. *Speaking for Ourselves: Autobiographical Sketches by Notable Authors of Books for Young Adults.* Urbana, IL: National Council of Teachers of English, 1990.

Bibliography

Bostrom, Kathleen Long. *Winning Authors: Profiles of Newbery Medalists.* Westport, CT: Libraries Unlimited, 2003.

Commire, Anne, ed. *Something About the Author: Facts and Pictures About Contemporary Authors and Illustrators of Books for Young People.* Vol. 134. Detroit, MI: Gale Group, Inc., 2003.

Gallo, Donald R., ed. *Speaking for Ourselves: Autobiographical Sketches by Notable Authors of Books for Young Adults.* Urbana, IL: National Council of Teachers of English, 1990.

Georgiou, Constantine. *Children and Their Literature.* Englewood Cliffs, NJ: Prentice-Hall, Inc., 1969.

Hoffman, Miriam, and Eva Samuels. *Authors and Illustrators of Children's Books: Writings on Their Lives and Works*. New York, NY: R. R. Bowker, 1972.

Hopkins, Lee Bennett. "Lee Bennett Hopkins Interviews Scott O'Dell." In *Star Walk*, by David P. Pearson et al. Needham, MA: Silver Burdett & Ginn, 1989.

Kingston, Carolyn T. *The Tragic Mode in Children's Literature*. New York, NY: Teacher's College Press, 1974.

Kirkpatrick, D. L., ed. *Twentieth-Century Children's Writers*. *2nd ed.* New York, NY: St. Martin's Press, 1983.

Laughlin, Jeannine L., and Sherry Laughlin. *Children's Authors Speak*. Englewood, CO: Libraries Unlimited, Inc., 1993.

Mahmoud, Lisa V., ed. *Books Remembered: Nurturing the Budding Writer*. New York, NY: Children's Book Council, 1997.

Meigs, Cornelia, Anne Thaxter Eaton, Elizabeth Nesbitt, and Ruth Hill Viguers. *A Critical History of Children's Literature: A Survey of Children's Books in English, Prepared in Four Parts under the Editorship of Cornelia Meigs*. *Rev. ed.* New York, NY: Macmillan Publishing Co., Inc., 1969.

O'Dell, Scott. *The Black Pearl.* New York, NY: Random House, 1996.

O'Dell, Scott. *Black Star, Bright Dawn.* Boston, MA: Houghton Mifflin Company, 1988.

O'Dell, Scott. *Country of the Sun: An Informal History and Guide.* New York, NY: Crowell, 1957.

O'Dell, Scott. *The Cruise of the Arctic Star.* Boston, MA: Houghton Mifflin Company, 1973.

O'Dell, Scott. *Island of the Blue Dolphins.* Boston, MA: Houghton Mifflin Company, 1960.

O'Dell, Scott. *The King's Fifth.* Boston, MA: Houghton Mifflin Company, 1966.

O'Dell, Scott. *Streams to the River, River to the Sea: A Novel of Sacagawea.* Boston, MA: Houghton Mifflin Company, 1986.

O'Dell, Scott. "The Tribulations of a Trilogy." *Horn Book Magazine*, April 1982.

Russell, David L. *Scott O'Dell.* New York, NY: Twayne Publishers, 1999.

Stewig, John Warren. "A Literary and Linguistic Analysis of Scott O'Dell's 'The Captive.'" Paper presented at the Annual Meeting of the National Conference on Language Arts in the Elementary School, Portland, OR, April 10–12, 1981.

Townsend, John Rowe. *A Sense of Story: Essays on Contemporary Writers for Children.* Philadelphia, PA: J. B. Lippincott Company, 1971.

Usrey, Malcolm. "Scott O'Dell," *American Writers for Children Since 1960: Fiction,* edited by Glenn E. Estes (Dictionary of Literary Biography). Detroit, MI: Gale Group, Inc., 1986.

Wintle, Justin, and Emma Fisher. *The Pied Pipers: Interviews with the Influential Creators of Children's Literature.* New York, NY: Paddington Press, Ltd., 1974.

Source Notes

Introduction

1. Donald R. Gallo, ed., *Speaking for Ourselves: Autobiographical Sketches by Notable Authors of Books for Young Adults* (Urbana, IL: National Council of Teachers of English, 1990), p. 154.
2. David L. Russell, *Scott O'Dell* (New York, NY: Twayne Publishers, 1999), p. 1.
3. John Rowe Townsend, *A Sense of Story: Essays on Contemporary Writers for Children* (Philadelphia, PA: J. B. Lippincott Company, 1971), p. 156.
4. Russell, p. 1.
5. Justin Wintle and Emma Fisher. *The Pied Pipers: Interviews with the Influential Creators of Children's Literature* (New York, NY: Paddington Press, Ltd., 1974), p. 176.

6. Russell, p. 99.
7. Townsend, p. 160.

Chapter 1

1. Donald R. Gallo, ed., *Speaking for Ourselves: Autobiographical Sketches by Notable Authors of Books for Young Adults* (Urbana, IL: National Council of Teachers of English, 1990), p. 154.
2. Scott O'Dell, *The Cruise of the Arctic Star* (Boston, MA: Houghton Mifflin Company, 1973), pp. 82–83.
3. Ibid., pp. 83–84.
4. Ibid., p. 84.
5. Ibid., pp. 100–101.
6. Lisa V. Mahmoud, ed., *Books Remembered: Nurturing the Budding Writer* (New York, NY: Children's Book Council, 1997), pp. 5–6.
7. Ibid., p. 5.
8. Ibid., p. 6.

Chapter 2

1. Donald R. Gallo, ed., *Speaking for Ourselves: Autobiographical Sketches by Notable Authors of Books for Young Adults* (Urbana, IL: National Council of Teachers of English, 1990), p. 154.
2. Ibid.
3. Ibid.
4. Ibid., pp. 154–155.
5. Jeannine L. Laughlin and Sherry Laughlin, *Children's Authors Speak* (Englewood, CO: Libraries Unlimited, Inc. 1993), p. 184.

6. David L. Russell, *Scott O'Dell* (New York, NY: Twayne Publishers, 1999), p. 15.

7. Scott O'Dell, *The Cruise of the Arctic Star* (Boston, MA: Houghton Mifflin Company, 1973), p. 161.

Chapter 3

1. Malcolm Usrey, "Scott O'Dell," *American Writers for Children Since 1960: Fiction*, edited by Glenn E. Estes, Dictionary of Literary Biography (Detroit, MI: Gale Group, Inc., 1986), p. 279.

2. David L. Russell, *Scott O'Dell* (New York, NY: Twayne Publishers, 1999), p. 26.

3. Lee Bennett Hopkins, "Lee Bennett Hopkins Interviews Scott O'Dell," in *Star Walk*, by David P. Pearson, et al. (Needham, MA: Silver Burdett & Ginn, 1989), p. 133.

4. Ibid., pp. 133–134.

5. Scott O'Dell, *Island of the Blue Dolphins* (Boston, MA: Houghton Mifflin Company, 1960), pp. 58–59.

6. Ibid., p. 65.

7. Ibid., pp. 67–68.

8. Ibid., p. 99.

9. Ibid., p. 153.

10. Carolyn T. Kingston, *The Tragic Mode in Children's Literature* (New York, NY: Teachers College Press, 1974), p. 148.

11. John Rowe Townsend, *A Sense of Story: Essays on Contemporary Writers for Children* (Philadelphia: J. B. Lippincott Company, 1971), p. 156.

12. Russell, p. 132.
13. Ibid., p. 31.
14. Townsend, p. 161.
15. Scott O'Dell, *The Cruise of the Arctic Star* (Boston, MA: Houghton Mifflin Company, 1973), p. 133.

Chapter 4
1. D. L. Kirkpatrick, ed., *Twentieth-Century Children's Writers*. 2nd ed. (New York, NY: St. Martin's Press, 1983), p. 157.
2. Scott O'Dell, *The King's Fifth* (Boston, MA: Houghton Mifflin Company, 1966), p. 263.
3. Malcolm Usrey, "Scott O'Dell," *American Writers for Children Since 1960: Fiction*, edited by Glenn E. Estes, Dictionary of Literary Biography. (Detroit, MI: Gale Group, Inc., 1986), p. 280.
4. Scott O'Dell, *The Black Pearl* (Boston, MA: Houghton Mifflin Company, 1967), p. 43.
5. Ibid., p. 56.
6. Ibid., p. 95.
7. Ibid., p. 95.
8. David L. Russell, *Scott O'Dell* (New York, NY: Twayne Publishers, 1999), p. 45.

Chapter 5
1. David L. Russell, *Scott O'Dell* (New York, NY: Twayne Publishers, 1999), p. 57.
2. Malcolm Usrey, "Scott O'Dell," *American Writers for Children Since 1960: Fiction*, edited by Glenn E. Estes, Dictionary of Literary Biography (Detroit, MI: Gale Group, Inc., 1986), p. 283.

3. Russell, p. 67.
4. Usrey, p. 286.
5. Jeannine L. Laughlin and Sherry Laughlin, *Children's Authors Speak* (Englewood, CO: Libraries Unlimited, Inc., 1993), p. 185.
6. Russell, p. 79.
7. Usrey, p. 291.
8. Anne Commire, ed., *Something about the Author: Facts and Pictures About Contemporary Authors and Illustrators of Books for Young People.* Vol. 134. (Detroit, MI: Gale Group, Inc., 2003), p. 118.
9. Lee Bennett Hopkins, "Lee Bennett Hopkins Interviews Scott O'Dell," in *Star Walk*, by David P. Pearson, et al. (Needham, MA: Silver Burdett & Ginn, 1989), p. 133.
10. Russell, p. 111.
11. Scott O'Dell, *Streams to the River, River to the Sea: A Novel of Sacagawea* (Boston, MA: Houghton Mifflin Company, 1986), p. 163.

Chapter 6

1. Anne Commire, ed., *Something about the Author: Facts and Pictures about Contemporary Authors and Illustrators of Books for Young People.* Vol. 134. (Detroit, MI: Gale Group, Inc., 2003), p. 117.
2. Lee Bennett Hopkins, "Lee Bennett Hopkins Interviews Scott O'Dell," in *Star Walk*, by David P. Pearson, et al. (Needham, MA: Silver Burdett & Ginn, 1989), p. 135.
3. Commire, p. 118.

4. Scott O'Dell, *The Cruise of the Arctic Star* (Boston, MA: Houghton Mifflin Company, 1973), p. xi.

5. David L. Russell, *Scott O'Dell* (New York, NY: Twayne Publishers, 1999), p. 84.

6. Malcolm Usrey, "Scott O'Dell," *American Writers for Children Since 1960: Fiction*, edited by Glenn E. Estes, Dictionary of Literary Biography (Detroit, MI: Gale Group, Inc., 1986), p. 292.

7. Hopkins, p. 136.

8. Russell, p. 98.

9. Scott O'Dell, *Black Star, Bright Dawn* (Boston, MA: Houghton Mifflin Company, 1988), p. 134.

Chapter 7

1. Lee Bennett Hopkins, "Lee Bennett Hopkins Interviews Scott O'Dell, in *Star Walk*, by David P. Pearson, et al. (Needham, MA: Silver Burdett & Ginn, 1989), p. 134.

2. Jeannine L. Laughlin and Sherry Laughlin, *Children's Authors Speak* (Englewood, CO: Libraries Unlimited, Inc., 1993), p. 183.

3. Hopkins, pp. 134–135.

4. H. K. Hall, "Scott O'Dell Award for Historical Fiction." Retrieved July 13, 2004 (http://www.scottodell.com/sosoaward.html).

5. John Rowe Townsend, *A Sense of Story: Essays on Contemporary Writers for Children* (Philadelphia, PA: J. B. Lippincott Company, 1971), p. 160.

6. Ibid., p. 161.

7. Ibid., p. 161.

8. Justin Wintle and Emma Fisher, *The Pied Pipers: Interviews with the Influential Creators of Children's Literature* (New York, NY: Paddington Press, Ltd., 1974), p. 173.
9. David L. Russell, *Scott O'Dell* (New York, NY: Twayne Publishers, 1999), p. 80.

Chapter 8

1. Donald R. Gallo, ed., *Speaking for Ourselves: Autobiographical Sketches by Notable Authors of Books for Young Adults* (Urbana, IL: National Council of Teachers of English, 1990), p. 155.
2. Miriam Hoffman and Eva Samuels, *Authors and Illustrators of Children's Books: Writings on Their Lives and Works* (New York, NY: R. R. Bowker, 1972), p. 347.
3. Jeannine L. Laughlin and Sherry Laughlin, *Children's Authors Speak* (Englewood, CO: Libraries Unlimited, Inc. 1993), p. 185.

Index

About the Author

Simone Payment has a degree in psychology from Cornell University and a master's degree in elementary education from Wheelock College. She is the author of nine books for young adults. Her book *Inside Special Operations: Navy SEALs* (also from the Rosen Publishing Group), won a 2004 Quick Picks for Reluctant Young Readers award from the American Library Association and is on the Nonfiction Honor List of Voice of Youth Advocates.

Photo Credits

Cover © Jim Kalett; p. 2 courtesy the Estate of Scott O'Dell.

Designer: Tahara Anderson; **Editor:** Nicholas Croce; **Photo Researcher:** Hillary Arnold